ELEVATORS

ELEVATORS

ELEVATORS

Rena Rosenwasser

KELSEY STREET PRESS   2011

Copyright © 2011 Rena Rosenwasser

ISBN: 978-0-932716-75-0
Library of Congress Control Number: 2010943234

Kelsey Street Press
2824 Kelsey St.
Berkeley, California 94705
Tel [510] 845-2260

info@kelseyst.com   www.kelseyst.com

Distributed by Small Press Distribution
[510] 524-1668   or   [800] 869-7553

FOR PENNY

CONTENTS

Triptych   11

Gurgling in the Monster Depths   17

Narrative Hesitates   23

Real Mummies Wait out the Hours   25

Structure Breaks   41

Storyville   49

Elevators   53

Triptych

Not to be undone. Not to be riddled with images. Or lost in compartments. Two floors up or on the ground. Stucco cracks in the middle of night and pieces fall. Sometimes I am sleeping when the falling happens.

I do not stir. What is familiar is my lover's hand undercover. She knows how to get to me when sleep is forgotten. Her small hands are long on exploration. That's why we like to travel. That's why we're here.

The mornings are full of speculation. I can sweep away the falling plaster. Doing it together is best. If easily. So we drive to Perugia. There are Peruginos in Perugia. There are Peruginos elsewhere. So we drive back.

Although there are two of us I am halted by thoughts of threes. I make three marks. Name three frescoes of Perugino I have not seen. Stretching myself, I cover sequences of words that fill three lines.

The house has the appearance of two floors. At least two inhabitable stories but if I extend myself I can see there is another floor below the two we are situated on. Is there a key somewhere that has eluded me?

What rules govern the traveler with only rudimentary knowledge of Italian? She can speak a little Italian. In the middle of the night spoken as screams of pleasure accompany further cracks in the surface.

Frescoes often are at peril. The most serious breaks of all. This afternoon in Montefalco there was a blank space in the story. Watching closely, I saw Umbria's own Francis had lost the detail, a void for a face.

Elsewhere he managed to hold up the walls of the cracked and falling church. The traveler steps back for a moment to look at the whole. The frescoes of Gozzoli fill the apse.

The saint seems to have gone everywhere. Enough tales for an entire dome. My memory can't hold the details of his story, only his lush buildings precede the surfaces of sleep.

Sometimes it is better to leave exposed places open. It is easier for the traveler to recognize what is missing. The absence of what was first placed there by whoever placed it there can be easily seen.

In the night exposed places draw attention. And they should. They were meant to be a source of distraction. How many ways touch them if folds in the cracks were further exposed to changes in the night air?

Two women ride on. They watch distant Umbrian hills fade away. A third woman's name is on a card that one of the two women has written. I read the name as the card slides back and forth along the narrow roads.

Here the only names that linger are of painters. All of these died over five hundred years ago. Except, that is, for Perugino. His pictures appear later. Fewer cracks where his stories locate themselves on walls.

Rules govern the nature of filling cracks. But how does the traveler know what's real and what isn't real? Who painted faces that she sees? My lover's face leads me to believe one more church is one too many.

How can I quit when I look up one more time and see another antique mass? Each stone leading me on. Is this the Romanesque or merely a Renaissance remodeling further confused by Baroque face-lifts?

Filling cracks. If the church made up for what's missing, we can speak of desire to keep splintered parts together. Did Francis converse with birds? Why was this story able to keep some medieval men from effacing others?

Commentary: Birds and trees of one hill town are much like those of another. For most viewers distinctions are not easily apparent. After several weeks I can hear a vast range between one bird call and the next.

Two women can think about this for a long time as they sit with arms at a slight distance from each other. Two glasses, one filled with Cynar, the other a bitter with a name that slips easily from the lover's lips.

Two women fill each other's glasses. There are no cracks in glasses
they arrange. They rearrange. In their fingers breadsticks crunch silence.
The sun is setting later and later and I like that it is.

Even in a hot sun glasses don't sweat. If they move toward each other,
they, not the glasses, will get hotter and hotter. The air is moister than
the air they remember in the place they usually inhabit.

The Umbrian birds with whom Francis spoke placed all relations in
another light. Who cares whether one place set siege to the next? The
birds will sound the same in any event, or if not then equally different.

Hill towns posed difficult problems to the medieval mind. To amplify
the height of what they were constructing medieval men built towers
so they could get a better view of the darkness coming towards them.

These views remain compelling. Our hands wander over each other
as we weave through narrow streets. Eyes find vicolos to gaze down
vistas where cultivated fields of olives and seeds of grano duro thrive.

Medieval passages recur. Every citadel had its arsenal of tricks.
The inhabitants of one keep would head for the ramparts and pour
hot oils on despised others crawling up their turrets.

Toppled towers are rarely available to travelers who want to view them.
It seems medieval minds often set them aflame. Deep in Perugia's bowels
we accidentally find ourselves captured at the base of the Baglioni tower.

Who knew when we read parcheggio and took the escalator up to centro
citta we would be inside a labyrinth of passageways scurrying from one
tower to the next. The medieval mind was given to elaborate schemes.

Stretches of the imagination darken as this infinite underground
protects us from the grey rainy day. I turn to capture my lover's eyes
for a moment before we decide to leap forward and of course up.

The Queen Mother is lunching in Perugia.
We discover the coo coo bird never sings until well into the afternoon,
or is this simply a chance happenstance in one locale?

Qualify the afternoon by a desire to render it with a little more light.
Less thunder. My lover likes it when she can recline, hold a biography
up against a background of Italian azure.

Later, hard rain. We hold darkness against the background. Our bodies
cold near thick stone walls. Sounds at a distance until we make them.
How creative can the passageway of voice be without sufficient light?

When falling happens I am sleeping. This time our Italian bed sinks when
least expected. I pull something out of the dream's background attempting
to hold onto blue malachite, familiar as I am with this fresco hue.

Restorations have provided the ideal shade. Returned color to its
origin. I have no desire to return to mine. Continue to wander through
Renaissance passageways. Pageant of costumes, painterly weaving.

Halos tooled with the intricacy of gold filigree. Narratives forced by a
clever hand. The brush of the period must have been a narrow one. Not
in the manner of the Renaissance but further back than that. Trecento.

What is rendered when everything has been restored? Lines are darkened
to distinguish eyes from flesh-toned face. Supposedly there is a protective
surface covering the invisible original marks.

The tourist likes to see what she has traveled to be reminded of. It seems
familiar though she has never seen the real thing. She is reminded further
the farther she looks. The restorer's hand aggravates the surface.

Who really made this? Difficult to imagine the original hand producing
the face that the traveler now sees. Better to stand back, squint, let the
colors alone return to their original vibrant pigment.

The silence of stone is a passageway. In the church better not to get too close to what she is trying to see. Waiting, she remembers the different marks with their confusing layers. Her feelings are not at all clear.

The tourist with her miniature camera that must never flash in the presence of frescoes. Something underneath the new surface, a surface she can barely see, might disintegrate. What was originally there, lost.

Perhaps it is already lost and what it is she thinks she sees is long since gone. Whose hand it is ascribed to has previously been erased. There is nothing underneath the overpainting.

She has this need to know. What is there and what is not there? An opening that lets the eye in to see more than original color. If a key could be found that turns easily and opens what is missing.

There are secrets that a place never gives up to the incidental traveler. There are mysteries that a lover likes to hold. What's underneath the surface has resonance. There are traces on the body as it says retrace me.

Kisses touch the cracks least exposed. They like a place where the line has no definition. Slippery is what they know. They lead the lover over the gaps that have no explanation.

Uncontrollable emanations occur where sacrifices are made. If the altar opens and only two of the three parts are visible. The desire for the invisible other appears to leak when least expected.

The designs of one panel are not necessarily the designs of the others. Even though they appear to have a lot in common. The colors are not all that different. What moves one of them usually moves all of them.

Out the encapsulated view there are clouds. Through the narrow window the Umbrian fields fill the stone room. I am wrestling with light in the visible absence of marks that used to be distant.

In the medieval background there is no view only gold leaf.
Triptychs contain these painted threads. A spiritual realm instead
of a landscape. Luminescence instead of what I've come to love.

Incandescent views where lovers hold each other's silence and look
at rows of narrow cypress. Rolling strands of green grey leaves are olives.
The distance fills. Easily. Three leaves unhinge.

Gurgling in the Monster Depths

WORDS TRANSGRESS.   Depart from their usual
fittings.   If I nudge them they might travel anywhere.

what queer   Rushing   Meaning   the riddle
is the other   that is illustrated

I was trying to   Adhere   in genderless

                                                    Site

the conjunction of being   writes
trust placed   lost footing

on a no longer   Identity slur
the flair   of hers him

Touch bottom   behind a mask
held   the body could

any position   How it un/held back

Amorphous forms alighted like film. Shapes gave up their names. Gender lost its essential glue. I was moving in and out of my substance as if I had numerous sleeves. I could choose among them & find a texture to desire. Dressing my arm I would fashion a self. Sometimes the self wore thin netting, sometimes it ventured out in curiously Baroque attire.

INDEFINITELY POSITIONED. curious.	The mutable self was It could dissolve its substance.
unguarded zone crossed	elastic impulses tightly
Constructed soft fruit Sequences	where Kiki's fake phalluses were flaccid
Everything make-believe	Mutable
	...*fruit of the loom* Everything
contends with fruit of the womb	
make-believe wanted touching Art	*was*

Invariably relationships could establish new sequences. Supple as I was I could edge into a space that was definitely not a white cube. There was more to this than just composition.

DESIRE'S BODY SLIPS.	Step across the unexpected folds.
An impulse to let my body slide	under and see how
shoulders might fit.	
I	erotically seized
by perpetual	displacement
of the Usual knowing/un knowing	Pleasure
negotiating an alternative position	Bandaged
my breast so tightly this breast/lessness	Let
this constriction	subjugate meaning
No, not to please	*anyone*
feigned mustache	the compulsion of
himness	brought my otherwise demure face
a licentiousness	to slide across
screens	
of sexual suitability	

This was possibly an entry … a perfect pause in which the pressure of the habitual lost its hold. I waited in silence for the excess cloth to reassemble. My silence paralleled the silence of those around me who sat in darkness watching images flicker. The fabric over me moved into place and the body underneath pushed arms and legs out of the available openings. All that remained was to pull the final zipper. I slowly moved and found myself in the opposite camp's skin.

BAROQUE IMPOSITION.	Neither seen nor said.
The carnivalesque	took up my head.
The Illustrated Woman	In extremis
Missed	the panels
How inside without a ticket	Myself a marginalia
Frankenstein's Daughters	*Talking Dirty*
How would pleasure	use form
of the particular	Woman pushed to pain
by the other when the other was woman	Playing
Man	though the woman at play
in perpetual flux after all	*a switch of*
positions	how unstable
is a metaphor of	Raw skin
was the woman	in the screening
Being a man	An open ended
Chain	Displaced
meaning inside me	a woman on her knees
licks the other woman's boots	Speak

Was this a game where every player knew her part? Here I was without a discourse. Their language hurled me onto an unfamiliar page. After all, *Frankenstein's Daughters* brought pictures onto the screen. Tenderness I'd always felt towards him ... in skirts these daughters brought tears to my eyes.

CONSTRUCTED PANORAMAS.   Narrative at this
precise moment.   Our monster dirndled slurs expected
lines

. . . something was   occurring

Sliding across   the blind girl
of the Classic version   warms to unseen bodies

with their new speech   furniture of early

film dissolves

I see   she can only hear
delicious gurgling   in the monster depths

Narrative Hesitates

drift   sleep's sheeted sounds   starched
perimeter
motion the bed round   *Father…*

Once upon a time   *fasten your ears to loose strands*
words repeated   close to the mouth   lips run on w/o any recognizable
surface syllables rush forward   a country where phonetics fragment

Never mind the continuous
present   sounds are counters fingers run faster tracks of syntax
tap tap   place w/o periods   hit the double space bar

Please   He says   *Prague*   he says…   (space) (space)   He
rushes on   *Budapest*

how crossed borders
spell Magyar   *Is there a place to sit*   benchmarks
tracks of syntax   syllables rush   over and over

Real Mummies Wait Out the Hours

There were awnings over my eyes
Why I needed to flip them

Or tell Shu who
every morning lifts the sun into the sky

A terribly bright situation

Who will mine limestone
climb pyramids?

Myriad steps

of Meidum

I tried scale
inner and irregular casing

lightly walk along
a wash
hike a line
with pull

palmed

rift

I pushed myself

Settlement   situation

⎴

STORY: Recounted by an 18th century Englishwoman who, upon visiting a mass grave in Egypt and breaking apart sections of the mummies, found *mommia* brown.

COLOR: *Mommia* was used by European painters to make shadows on canvas.... Mummy brown made from the ancients themselves... out of gummy liquor that exuded from embalmed flesh. A thick bitumen-like substance with a hue somewhere between burnt and raw umber.

Measurement risen from flat

Planes

Pyramids

Scribe, scribbler of lists
Vizier, judge

He who watches over
      maker
           of monuments

    Luxor, where the sun slithers into the nether world
& gaze goes west to where the dead were buried

The archaeologist reads   *The Coffin Text*

those who have gone to their Ka
while Ba souls remain

Now all at once

A mummy, a murmur

Frontier
Far off the felucca   we went to Philae

In my thought
conflating Flaubert's

    corporeal

visions of the bizarre
fugitive

veiled woman in the
distant   Oasis

Synchronicity
    saints
 sit
in my hands

        touch Ptolemy

  temple

verticals lift
on the East side   Nile
Aswan

quarry
boat

float
up river

Imagine obelisks here at the fourth cataract, the archaeologist motions
   transported all the way to Luxor

          simply
souls of the dead

                    Ba souls unite with their
mummies

Did the female Pharaoh come down this far?

Time is a snake
Scarab red

Egyptians called the island Biak   island at the end

      now   Elephantine

or we sip
sit
  Colonial bar

iced tea urgent something
    & sugary
      Egyptian sweet
        the other day

What was it?

Oommm   ma   la

SITUATION I

On the west side
were the dead
themselves

as I walk the streets of the Old Quarter
Al Jazeera's news
sounds

pressure
of the present
implodes

a Bedouin's bombed
the old bazaar of Sharm el-Sheikh

In the tomb

      it is painted
the drowned will float in the 10th hour

Every day the dead voyage through 12 hours
of night

each evening Nut swallows the sun
  her stretched arms and elongated legs
              light travels through her body

in cut caverns
blue black sky

flesh-toned stars

if you were to exert physical effort

the archaeologist says,
Climb over to Deir-el-Bahri

*See stairs flaunted on each end
by granite Sphinx*

*Here on the other side of the Valley of Kings
her Temple
the Pharaoh Hatshepsut*

    she fishes and fowls with gods.

        In the fresco
wears crowns of Upper and
Lower Egypt

Her envoys on a trading mission to Punt
carry gifts, baboons, panthers, incense

Float

Up the Nile

back and down

In her temple hear

   Book of the Heavenly Cow
(spoken cow another form of Nut)

All these volumes
     Netherworlds

If the sun should sit between 2 horns is
it that Hathor holds the sun?

How heavy is
Obelisk?

⌐⌐⌐

Belzoni lifted

Lifted the contents
Lifted a lot of his Kunstkammer
Ancient wonder

Eyelid of malachite
gilded bed

Shallow Nile

navigate
causeway, chapel to East

sed-complex

the moment

I looked out
    on the uninhabited
      & Elephantine place

earlier Egyptian thoughts now
uttered, *inshallah*

in Arabic
Ipsambul

Situated
Unnatural haunt   a Souk
    how far the bazaar
Bedouin baskets

Red peppers   *shah*
Shata in bright mounds

‾‾‾⌐‾⌐‾‾‾

In the 6th hour of the *Book of Gates*

Ra   big as Belzoni   uncovering the Door

Lifted block
Monument

Seti I   1st of the Rameses

In the 6th hour of the *Book of...*

Sarcophagus

Apex
Sneferu
Khufu

Did they use ramps?

Was there a smooth outer shell
quarried from Tufa?

The photographer whose tripod slips

& unseals   then say *go*
12 steps down

vertical passageway

find...
wrapped in reed: 3 legs of a bull
crushed horned skull, & 2 wine jugs

reminder

remains

gilded carrying chair

Mother of Khufu

Was this your bracelet of lapis?

Mother of Khufu
Hetepheres

Perfectly balanced

Alabaster

Find
canopic chests
full
Unopened seal
compartments—
solutions of natron and water,
another dried organic material

But her mummy is missing

Where is the missing mummy?

SITUATION II

Mother of Khufu

Hovering line

where we dine
A dozen Sheiks convene

A veiled woman alone
& eating
only a slit for lips
sealed mouth

food pushed

      linen
strips   Bela Lugosi
    cloak

filmic moments

unravel

synchronicity

   standing in the mummy room
 Museum

where temperature's cool
cooler than any place in Lower Egypt

     the only perfectly chilled site

here Cairo far from blare of film monitors
in the Museum where everything is

real mummies wait out hours
on horizontal tablets

Structure Breaks

where expected	Sleep
fell the familiar crumbled	Suddenly
susceptible to my missing part	Texture no longer
gripped	an essential hold
Penetrated by night	the void
of enamel depth	distinguished from earlier primates
Gaps	in the tendency
Missing nothing now links	a Southern fossil left
the Sudan	with a former strategy
evolutionary matter	Works

The exotic woman speaks English. Skin covers her foreignness in a distant linen. Verbs motion inside her mouth. We climb up and down stairs in the multilevel house. Her arms cycle madly navigating the space surrounding her body. We venture out among the dimly lit streets. Transients accost us, break into her stories, grabbing her wrists. Without hesitation, she slips bracelets down her arms and casts them away. Dazzled by the ease of her gesture, my thoughts cross the terrain of her glittering materials. The jewels were luminous set against her skin. Suddenly her husband appears. People gather around him. She and he vibrate, communicating in an incomprehensible language. He has many lovers, one a young blond man. The husband is a dervish whirling to arouse attention. She ignores the gyrations. We venture up the staircase. I am riveted to her every turn. Clearly she desires something: she says, *Come, let's go with this!* Propelled by these riddles I rise up the stairs, *What about him? Never mind*, she says. My eyes run down her arms. There is gravity to the lightness in my body. Her tongue carves words. Silvery gestures up and down my throat.

Antiquity slips. The memory of a body moves into me. Lost heat recaptures the body's dense field. She leans over me. What I don't really say she can't see. Her silvery tangents have led me to where I am driven. The missing jewels have long since vanished. Under her texture I wander like a spindle. Her tongue ululating inside my surface. I'm thrown before sound's arrival into soundlessness. Desire is a window out of which I once more see my former self. Reaching for this self, a furious image breaks the sequence. The dreamer dreaming interrupts the fluid body's sense. A tooth stood before me. It was maimed; it was mine. I could feel the textural specificity of rapid disintegration. Crumbling buildings, the scent of dust. I stood in the shadow of what was once a stable fixture. A gap took hold that threw me out of sequence. The dance of the rising stairs no longer touched its verbs. Loss was the language that now fed the rush toward decomposition.

Possibility of meat	Fixed reach
not the site of sleep	more substantially
I never find myself eating anything	real when dreaming
If I step on a slippery surface	speak the
word *green*	
I might visit a Southern place	let thought
gather fossils	the desert's Agave
permeates my sleeping I	& spinach unable to root
often plausibility	skis on sand

Rift in locale or dreams place capability. The exact nectar when no other juice sufficed. There was a girl who had a problem. She seemed to be perfect except she ran into a tree. The tree was harder than stone. Could this possibly be an accident? Or was there something wrong with the perfect girl? In the dream she had esoteric abilities. She was capable of distracting others from hesitancy. But there she was, a curious subject, though small in proportions. She was smiling and holding onto her mother's long skirts. When she let go of the material all eyes followed her. She ran and ran through the fertile terrain, except that she didn't get anywhere. Her appearance was that of a small female who was stunned unconscious. Standing at a distance I stared and watched as the mother lifted the child's body.

The scene changed before I could move forward. Though my thoughts stayed behind and worried over the fate of the fallen girl. Was she alive, even though she had been removed from the scene? Was she inside the frame of another sequence? The same dream but a later chapter. Vestige of the fear of loss lingering inside a new occasion.

no shelf to stand on	needed lift
sequential leap	how high pillow's sea
	on an otherwise Aegean
null	ness
not just any flotilla	weaving sheep
spindle	shore
a line	combs

Readers and dreamers share susceptibility to bodily displacement. She reads me a story woven in wool. The tale softens in her telling ... a boat is rocking. The point is passed where heels grasp certain ground. Senses roam over where she reads. Pageants that she sees and says were there are there in her tales of painted boats. The boats inside her narratives have long narrow hulls. She says, *It's time,* they say, *here somewhere past the Neolithic where the Bronze Age hasn't reached.* Islands are like that, secluded from extremes. Men are off on the Aegean trading while women tend looms and gardens. Lily and saffron crocus offer stamens for the picking. Murex and madder, dyes they fix with mineral alum. Spirals of hearts are set point to point. Intricacy is a labyrinth. Theirs is an economy of textiles. They weave waves with rosettes & yellow lozenges like diamonds.

A labyrinth that was might have gone on. Readers of narratives know what moves forward falters in a sudden eruption. A volcano's pressure shifts all expected relations. The story stops when a blur occurs over our Mediterranean site. Later the seeming relationship will find its archaeologist to establish sequence. The displaced location will have its sifter and its sieve. To be trapped under ash means to leave no fabric. A textileless-ness haunts these labyrinths. Shards will carry narratives as frescoes reassemble. Paint marks threads of woven removal.

Night walks over me. Dreams concur. Inhabitants negotiate motion across fields. Attention goes there, to arrangement. There is no easy rest if it isn't right. Eyes assemble as thought opens gardens. The palpable landscapes are highly contained. They seem natural but are actually painstakingly composed. The dreamer's brain constructs an ideal ephemeral from actual matter. Innumerable panicles walk through sleep. I venture in a paradise where my mind watches itself walking over mounds of tufted grass. An engagement with so much ease it is as if I carried the composition of home in these mental easements. There are other women who situate themselves among the flowers in my dream; they point to individual beds held together by precise arrangements. Each bed contains its own formal pleasure. I am conscious of these perfect places where I might have been or never was.

textured relationships	grasp how we
fragment	where story
encourages relationship	elements make decisions
desire strongly present	escapes quickly
assertion's substance	waking
what isn't	what is

Storyville

Alice returned often to the numbered avenues that ran the length of her island. Just a small sliver of sky rested between the facades of its tall buildings. Alice was always walking up and down the city's corridors. All her life she had felt a sense of clarity from this urban measure, which resonated brightly, like sound in a canyon. From the moment she had first come out of the nebulous space of the outer boroughs into the city, the city electrified her.

After the E train doors closed shut she climbed from the depths of the subway to natural light. From there it was easy to find a proper gait. The anonymity Storyville provided suited her. Striding downtown everything opened before her. What could hold more promise than to ascend the stairs of the great library! She called up books and let the printed pages swallow her impulses.

There were other public buildings in which she could lose herself by entering through revolving glass doors. One of her favorites was just off Fifth. Inside it was spacious and oil paintings hung on the walls. Few people were there and she could easily walk through rooms organized by art movements. History also had a hand in the heightened awareness but words were beside the point. It was looking that spoke to her in texture, volume, hue, and intensity. A painting by a man with a Russian name might frighten her, but she would extend her gaze beyond the branches to the vivid hues, and then feel carried beyond fear. Another by a French man had thin-brushed washes of color. A man played a violin and two women lightly clothed were in each other's arms. Alice imagined figures dancing to Diaghilev's pronouncements —fauns and bright birds crisscrossed. Sometimes colors were enclosed by line and sometimes brushstrokes moved without defining lines. Color might be a wash or thickly caked with distinct brushstrokes.

Bristles with paint danced across fields Alice longed to inhabit. Could she imagine the hand behind the brush moving smoothly or dabbing and jerking across the surface? These thoughts released her from the normal chatter of her days. Usually pressures would envelop her from morning to night. She always fell short. How could she go from A to B in a linear progression, if everyone expected this movement? Alice never knew what was going to happen next.

When others watched, it was as if Alice could not perform in the way others expected. The city was her escape. Here in the avenues, clouds were caught as if hyperventilating between tall buildings. There was always this intense *Wow* factor!

There were other diversions, more mainstream, that she could share with friends. In the museum, downstairs, away from the exhibits, they would go into a theater, where old films played. On the screen were projected images. A character in one, Ninotchka, took them to Paris where she tried on hats. Everyone was in black and white and spoke English with fake Russian accents. One day a woman walked into the theater and sat in their row. She wore a wide brimmed hat and looked terribly familiar, though older.

Often when Alice waited too long to return home to the outer boroughs she would be pressed on all sides by passengers. In the underground, this was the way one left the city at the end of the day, standing and looking, though never daring to look directly into anyone's eyes, which was considered a terrible form of trespass.

~ ~ ~

For a year now Alice had kept herself on a strict regime. All her focus had been on internal changes. The narratives that were of concern had to do with excretion of cells and fluids. Time was either wholly in the present or tumbling backwards—so many things that were important to her had happened in the city of her childhood. It had been a locus of possibility. There she had not needed to be so small in her thoughts.

Figures that had once captivated her on canvas now gave way to a passion for abstraction: pencilled grids on canvas or painted surfaces filled with washes of color. What was it, she thought, if the field of the painting moved outward into a horizonless space?

~ ~ ~

When the last and tallest of the buildings on the island was made everyone had apparently come to a consensus that some other direction was needed. It no longer seemed elegant or even industrious to keep the old game of verticality in play. Verticality for its own sake had vanished. The grid was great but tall was not. Keep the horizon intact. Multiple floors no longer meant solidity; in the news Alice read the buildings were so tall that of course they were perfect targets. A new solution was called for. There would be meetings, councils. The city had always been called New. Some critics said it had lost its freshness.

These opinions seemed to be beside the point, though the papers were full of them. Returning to her city, Alice let her eyes re-enter familiar corridors of light; everything she once felt became tangible again. Walking the avenues, staring uptown past the Flatiron building, or the one named after a car, cumulus clouds and shafts of light came into view. Narrow grey buildings framed billowing whites and cerulean blues. Alice felt life itself wedged there between these imposing stone structures.

She moved through rooms whose dimensions had been altered. When she stood before familiar paintings feelings radiated inside her almost like pulses. She was surrounded by throngs of visitors and it took more maneuvering to make her way forward, but once she reached the paintings, the beats would pound inside her and reverberate outwards.

Expansion of the universe, which she had read about in the Science supplement, concerned a shift towards the red: the wavelength of light was increasing as space enlarged and thus objects were moving farther and farther apart. Ruminating on redness brought her beside one of her favorite works, *Broadway Boogie Woogie.* There she stood for an extended stretch. There was so much dissonance around, including people with audio devices, that she had to concentrate a long time to reduce it to an intensely low hum.

Elevators

Skyscraper
Fire-resistant steel
How I spent the afternoon
turning Eiffel's bridge vertical   Possible   plumb-

referent-
line

call me *the machine that makes the land*
pay

or take the rococo of Chrysler

Manhatta
the name   perhaps a tall horse
or the uppermost sail
of a ship

This harbor of Manhatta
was born

The century begins here and where will it end

After the new one began we were delirious and so we took to the train

It went as far as the follies

of Luna Park

Coney Island is an island apart from Manhatta

Electric lights on Roebling's bridge

The city

From the top from above. We can see
time ticking

all the way to
Canal Street

Everyone knows
from above

from afar

order
trade. Mathematical conjecture for

more

Metropolis

Manhatta's grid

13 avenues run up and down
a hundred and fifty-five streets sweep across
pure potential
    in fact, it is the most courageous act of prediction in Western civilization: the land it divides, unoccupied; the population it describes, conjectural; the buildings it locates, phantoms; the activities it frames, nonexistent.

  In the harbor
everyday was everywhere...

    *Materials here under your eye shall change their shape as if
        by magic...*

Everything imagined was lit
lit later not now

how we took measure
              of goods, machinery, steam.

where having

With latest connections, works, the inter-transportation of
    the world...
This earth all spann'd with iron rails, with lines...

Of grid   grid'd
steel possible
possibly   cabled

Otis (of course)

The lift would hold
all of us up

A height if you've got it right
try me in the guise of the gauge

In excessive measures of coated steel

When my body goes up
Everyone else is left behind

The century begins

Who's counting
anyway?

For Woolworth's sake
more floors than any before
gild the Gothic with nickels and dimes

Tallest in the world
Spandrels, pinnacles and piers   the exterior thrust

Floors
fabric the infinite

Taller than the gilded realms

Still the exterior surface just a light skin—

Precision   translucence
metaphysical urgency   my eye moving

Louis Sullivan leaps through clear grids
shimmering horizontals
skeletal vertical

How night
flickering light

City
without limits

I was born

                                Pulling you
                                      something   subterranean depth

          I wanted to hold onto up, space of the
          future, new building
          You
          stirring   under the surface
          last and lost

          down
          pavement

          Concrete residuals

You want to go faster   under

                                          the subway
                             senses flying forward

pictures moving
everything impossible possibly so

You'd never seen a *Daily News*

THE INTERIOR IS THE CITY WITHIN THE SELF

Who would have ever imagined
in augmentation
rising
high

as if we had taken Coney Island
home

in our mind's eye
forward was rushing up

                                                                                    & you would open the door of the caged

                                                                                   elevator into imagined
                                                                                    rooms

        now more real than the Crystal Palace

Or the towers of a far flung Exposition
Was it Paris or Philadelphia? Had we walked the Elysian
champs
of that other city

Was it an ancienne ville… or a simple burg?

EIFFEL IMAGINES ELEVATED PLACES

For the First Universal Exposition, when they called on Gustave
to build the tallest tower

How long did it take?

Only 21 months to steal the show

Vertical leaps

until Broad Street led to Broad
way

&
ah   so simple
called   Flatiron

Just that
perfect
two streets come together
and touch

Like you they have only three sides

Industrial urgency

emergent iron
Flagg's   Little Singer
wrought, cast of green sewing
... a rat tat tat of machines

Sewing

When we roam our own   Nouveau

York
join me

let the platforms rise

SOURCES & ACKNOWLEDGMENTS:

TRIPTYCH

Grateful acknowledgment to *Zyzzyva*, where an earlier version of the poem appeared.

REAL MUMMIES WAIT OUT THE HOURS

Giovanni Belzoni (the 'Patagonian Samson') was the first modern European to visit Egypt's Valley of the Kings. Sponsored in 1816 by Henry Salt, English Consul-General in Egypt, Belzoni is credited with the discovery of the tombs of Ramesses I and Seti I. His strength allowed him to remove colossal treasures from the ancient tombs.

ELEVATORS

page 53   Cass Gilbert's definition of a skyscraper, *New York's 50 Best Skyscrapers*, Eric Nash, City and Company, 1997

page 55 (first quote)   Rem Koolhaas describing the formation of the 1811 grid that created Manhattan, *Delirious New York*, Monacelli Press, 1994

pages 55 (second quote), 56   Walt Whitman, "Song of the Exposition," *The Complete Poems of Walt Whitman*, Penguin Classics, 2004

MY DEEPEST GRATITUDE FOR THEIR EYES AND ENCOURAGEMENT:

Mei-mei Berssenbrugge, Ramsay Breslin, Kate Delos, Patricia Dienstfrey, Amber DiPietra, Barbara Guest, Thalia Kitrilakis, Hazel White and Valerie Witte

Colophon

Elevators is a limited edition of 750 copies.
Cover art by Richard Tuttle.
Design by Poulson/Gluck and Robert Rosenwasser.
Cover text is set in Invicta and Helvetica.
Interior text is set in Bodoni Classic, with titles in Helvetica Light.

Kelsey Street Press 2011

About the Author

Rena Rosenwasser grew up in New York City where she cultivated her passion for literature and the visual arts. After graduating from Sarah Lawrence College in 1971, she moved to California to pursue graduate studies at Mills College, Oakland, where she earned her MA in literature in 1976. In 1974 she settled in Berkeley, where she co-founded Kelsey Street Press and subsequently served as its longtime director.

Initially the press's mission was simply to publish women writers, who were marginalized by small and mainstream publishers. As poets took up the challenge of feminism and the language poets, the press placed more emphasis on innovative writing practices. Between 1987 and 2006, Rosenwasser initiated and produced a series of collaborations between poets and visual artists that established Kelsey Street as the premiere and longest lived independent publisher of literature for women.

Rosenwasser's poetry publications include *Dittany (Taking flight)* (Mayacamas Press, 1993); *Unplace.Place* (Leave Books, 1992); and three collaborations with artist Kate Delos: *Isle* (Kelsey Street Press, 1992); *Aviary* (Limestone Press, 1988); and *Simulacra* (Kelsey Street Press, 1986). Her first volume of poetry, *Desert Flats*, was published by Kelsey Street Press in 1979.

Currently a board member of Small Press Distribution, Rosenwasser has also served on the Literary Panel for the California Arts Council. Together with her partner, Penny Cooper, she travels extensively and supports and collects the work of contemporary women artists.

Photo: Lynda Koolish